Disney · PIXAR
Art Studio
Project Book

THUNDER BAY
P · R · E · S · S
San Diego, California

Thunder Bay Press
An imprint of Printers Row Publishing Group
A division of Readerlink Distribution Services, LLC
10350 Barnes Canyon Road, Suite 100, San Diego, CA 92121
www.thunderbaybooks.com

Printers Row Publishing Group is a division of Readerlink Distribution Services, LLC. The Thunder Bay Press name and logo are trademarks of Readerlink Distribution Services, LLC.

All notations of errors or omissions should be addressed to Thunder Bay Press, Editorial Department, at the above address. All other correspondence (author inquiries, permissions) concerning the content of this book should be addressed to Walter Foster Publishing, a division of Quarto Publishing Group USA Inc., 6 Orchard Road, Suite 100, Lake Forest, CA 92630.

Publisher: Peter Norton

ISBN: 978-1-62686-530-3

Made in Shenzhen, China.

19 18 17 16 15 1 2 3 4 5

Disney · PIXAR
Art Studio
Project Book

Table of Contents

Tools and Materials

SKETCHING PENCIL

The sketching pencil in this kit has an HB lead hardness. This pencil won't smear easily like soft pencils do or scratch the surface of watercolor paper like hard pencils.

COLORED PENCILS

This kit contains seven colored pencils. Be sure to store them in the kit or a separate container. The lead in a colored pencil is brittle and likely to break inside the shaft if the pencil is dropped. This may not be immediately apparent, but will eventually render the pencil useless.

FINE-TIPPED BLACK MARKER

Use the fine-tipped black marker to ink your drawings. You can also experiment with ink, brush, dip, and ballpoint pens for different effects. Whenever possible, work with black waterproof ink for more permanent results.

SHARPENER

You can achieve various effects depending on how sharp or dull your pencil is, but generally you'll want to keep your pencils sharp. A sharp point will provide a smooth layer of color.

KNEADED ERASER

The success of erasing colored pencil marks depends on two main factors: the color of the pencil line and the amount of pressure that was applied. Darker colors tend to stain the paper, making them difficult to remove, and heavy lines are difficult to erase, especially if the paper's surface has been dented.

WATERCOLOR PAINTS

This kit contains three watercolor paints in tubes. Watercolor paints are commonly available in three forms—tubes, pans, and cakes. Most artists prefer tubes because the paint is already moist and mixes easily with water.

PAINTBRUSHES

Many paintbrush styles are available, but two are most commonly used with watercolor—flat brush and round brush. A flat brush has bristles of equal length that produce even strokes. A round brush has bristles that taper to a point, which allows it to hold a good amount of water. You can also vary your pressure on the brush to create a variety of stroke widths.

PALETTE

The plastic palette in this kit features several wells for pooling and mixing your watercolors. It's easily cleaned with soap and water.

Colored Pencil Basics

HOLDING THE PENCIL

The way you grip the pencil directly impacts the strokes you create. Some grips will allow you to press more firmly on the pencil, resulting in dark, dense strokes. Others hinder the amount of pressure you can apply, rendering lighter strokes. Still others give you greater control over the pencil for creating fine details. Experiment with each of the grips below.

Photos © Quarto Publishing Group

Underhand Grip By cradling the pencil, you control it by applying pressure only with the thumb and index finger. This grip can produce a lighter line. Your whole hand should move (not just your wrist and fingers).

Conventional Grip For the most control, grasp the pencil about 1½" from the tip. Hold it the same way you write, with the pencil resting firmly against your middle finger. This grip is perfect for smooth applications of color, as well as for making hatch strokes and small, circular strokes.

Overhand Grip Guide the pencil by laying your index finger along the shaft. This is the best grip for strong applications of color made with heavy pressure.

PRESSURE

Your main tool for darkening the color with colored pencils is the amount of pressure you use. It is always best to start light so that you maintain the tooth (or the texture of roughness or smoothness) of the paper for as long as possible.

Light Pressure Here, color was applied by whispering a sharp pencil over the paper's surface. With light pressure, the color is almost transparent.

Medium Pressure This middle range creates a good foundation for layering.

Heavy Pressure Pushing down on the pencil flattens the paper's texture, making the color appear almost solid.

Watercolor Basics

Watercolor paint straight from the tube is generally too dry and thick to work with, so you'll need to dilute it with water. The less water you use, the more intense the color will be.

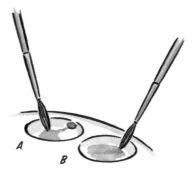

Starting Out Small Watercolors are very concentrated—a little goes a long way. Start by squeezing out a pea-sized amount of paint into one of the wells of your mixing palette.

Diluting the Paint Dip your brush in clean water, and then mix the water with the paint. Keep adding water until you achieve the dilution level you want (A). You can also transfer some of the paint to a separate well for mixing with other colors or for diluting the paint further (B).

Dilution Chart Here's how brilliant red looks in four different dilution levels, from slightly diluted to very diluted.

TESTING YOUR COLORS
It's always a good idea to have a piece of scrap paper handy to test your colors before applying them to your painting.

Color Basics

Color can help bring your drawings to life, but first it helps to know a bit about color theory. There are three *primary* colors: red, yellow, and blue. These colors cannot be created by mixing other colors. Mixing two primary colors produces a *secondary* color: orange, green, and purple (or violet). Mixing a primary color with a secondary color produces a *tertiary* color: red-orange, red-purple, yellow-orange, yellow-green, blue-green, and blue-purple. Reds, yellows, and oranges are "warm" colors; greens, blues, and purples are "cool" colors.

THE COLOR WHEEL

A color wheel is useful for understanding relationships between colors. Knowing where each color is located on the color wheel makes it easy to understand how colors relate to and react with one another.

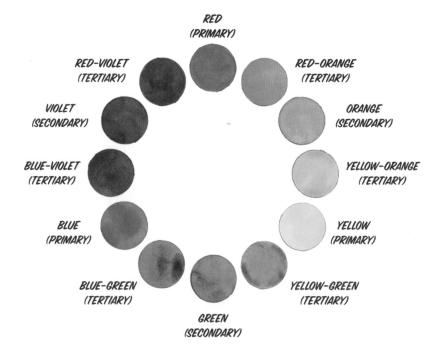

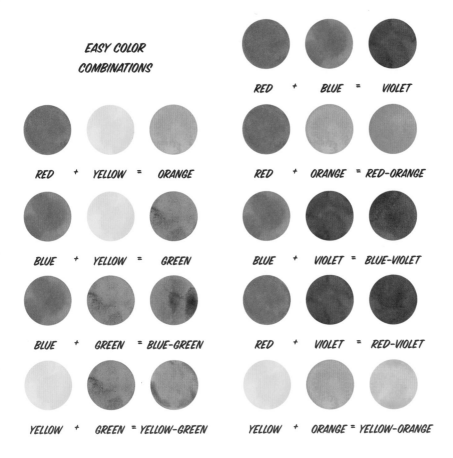

EASY COLOR COMBINATIONS

RED + BLUE = VIOLET

RED + YELLOW = ORANGE

RED + ORANGE = RED-ORANGE

BLUE + YELLOW = GREEN

BLUE + VIOLET = BLUE-VIOLET

BLUE + GREEN = BLUE-GREEN

RED + VIOLET = RED-VIOLET

YELLOW + GREEN = YELLOW-GREEN

YELLOW + ORANGE = YELLOW-ORANGE

BLENDING COLORED PENCILS

Colored pencils are transparent by nature, so instead of "mixing" colors as you would for painting, you create blends directly on the paper by layering colors on top of one another.

ADDING COLOR TO YOUR DRAWING

Some artists draw directly on illustration board or watercolor paper and then apply color directly to the original pencil drawing; however, if you are a beginning artist, you might opt to preserve your original pencil drawing by making several photocopies and applying color to a photocopy. This way, you'll always have your original drawing in case you make a mistake or you want to experiment with different colors or mediums.

How to Use This Book

Usually artists draw characters in several steps. Sometimes the steps are different, depending on what you're drawing. The important thing to remember is to start simply and add details later. The blue lines show each new step, and the black lines show what you've already drawn.

1

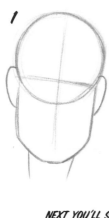

THE FIRST THING YOU'LL DRAW ARE GUIDELINES TO HELP POSITION THE FEATURES OF THE CHARACTER.

2

NEXT YOU'LL START TO ADD DETAILS TO YOUR DRAWING. IT WILL TAKE MULTIPLE STEPS TO ADD ALL OF THE DETAILS.

3

4

WHEN YOU FINISH ALL THE
DETAILS OF YOUR DRAWING,
YOU'LL GO BACK AND ERASE
YOUR GUIDELINES. YOU CAN
ALSO DARKEN YOUR LINES WITH
A PEN OR MARKER.

5

NOW CREATE YOUR OWN
COLORED VERSION!

Carl Fredricksen

Carl Fredricksen is a shy 78-year-old who wishes people would leave him alone. Each morning Carl meticulously vacuums every surface and straightens every doily, making sure things are just as his beloved late wife, Ellie, left them. After his morning cleaning ritual, Carl eats the same breakfast he's eaten every day for the past 50 years. Then he puts on his hat, sits on his porch, and glares at people talking too loudly into their newfangled portable phones as they walk by.

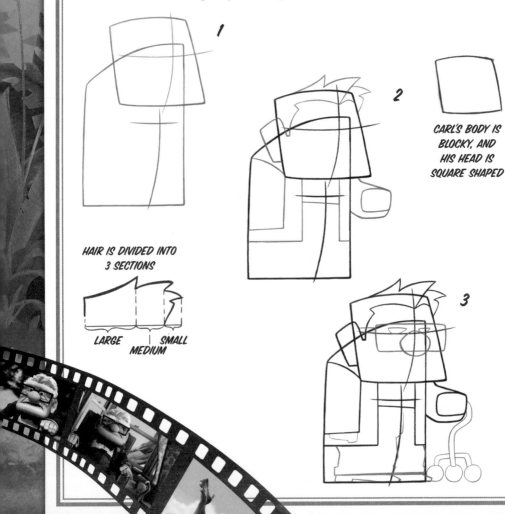

1

2

CARL'S BODY IS BLOCKY, AND HIS HEAD IS SQUARE SHAPED

HAIR IS DIVIDED INTO 3 SECTIONS

LARGE | MEDIUM | SMALL

3

4

5

6

FINGERS ARE BLOCKY

7

START WITH SQUARE GLASSES

CUT IN FOR NOSE

Russell

Russell is Carl Fredricksen's neighbor. He has enough gear to make him the most prepared 8-year-old Junior Wilderness Explorer in Explorer history. The only problem is, he's never been anywhere except the Camping Museum downtown. Determined to get his "Assisting the Elderly" badge and be promoted to Senior Wilderness Explorer, Russell's dream is to attend the father-son ceremony so his dad can pin on Russell's new badge. First, Russell must hound Carl Fredricksen with assistance—even if it means following Carl to the ends of the globe and back.

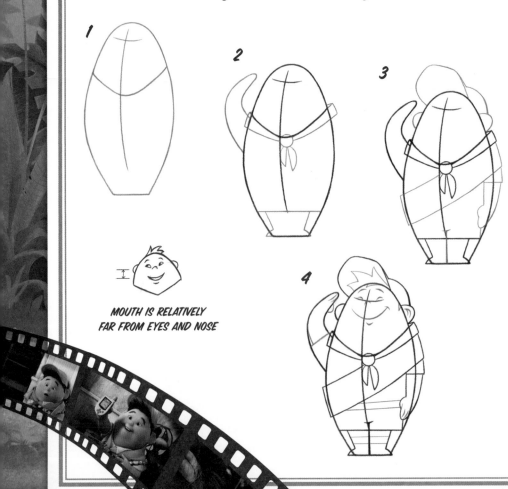

MOUTH IS RELATIVELY FAR FROM EYES AND NOSE

5

6

BODY IS
ROUGHLY EGG
SHAPED

7

START WITH SIMPLE
FLIPPER-LIKE ARMS;
THEN ADD FINGERS

Carl's House

Carl loves the home he shared with Ellie because it is filled with many happy memories of their life together. When Carl is ordered out of his house, he seizes the opportunity to fulfill Ellie's lifelong dream of living at Paradise Falls in South America. Carl ties thousands of balloons to his house, climbs inside, and escapes up into the clouds on an exciting adventure!

5

6

SQUARE OBJECTS REPRESENT CARL;
ROUND OBJECTS REPRESENT ELLIE.
THE ROOF HAS A BLEND OF SHAPES
TO SHOW THAT THE HOUSE IS A PART
OF BOTH OF THEM.

7

ONLY DRAW A
FEW BRICKS ON
THE CHIMNEY.
IT'S EASIER
AND HAS THE
SAME EFFECT!

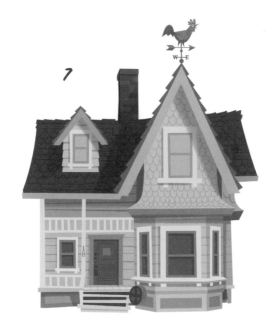

Kevin

Named by Russell, Kevin is a 12-foot-tall flightless jungle bird whom Russell sets free from a trap. Forever grateful, Kevin—a female—follows Russell and Carl on their adventure.

EYES STARE STRAIGHT OUT — THEY DO NOT POINT IN A SPECIFIC DIRECTION

 YES!

 NO!

KEVIN IS BIG COMPARED TO CARL AND RUSSELL

4

5

HEAD FEATHER HAS A
BULB-LIKE END

6

7

TO LOOK DOWN, SHE
TURNS HER HEAD IN
FUNNY ANGLES

Dug

Dug is a desperate dog who wants nothing more than to be part of a pack. Because of a technological invention, Dug can verbally communicate with humans. Unfortunately, this talking device doesn't help Dug much in the "brains" department, but he'll do anything to make his master happy. Dug must decide who deserves his loyalty—the pack he's known his entire life or this new pack with Carl and Russell.

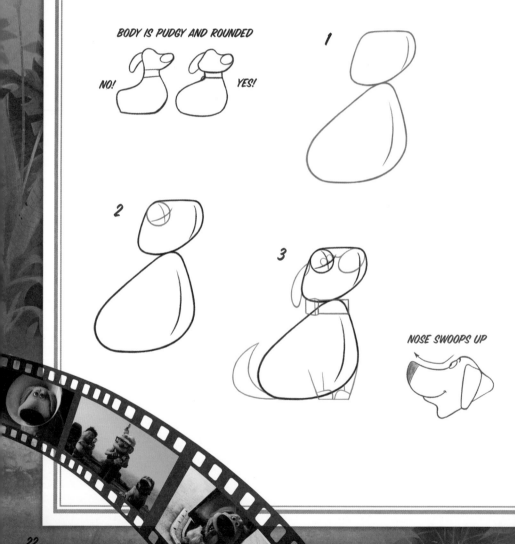

BODY IS PUDGY AND ROUNDED

NO!   YES!

1

2

3

NOSE SWOOPS UP

4

5

6

7

TAIL FUR
FLARES
MOST IN
THE MIDDLE

PAWS ARE SMALL
COMPARED TO BODY

SKETCH HERE!

Merida

Merida is the adventurous Princess of DunBroch. More comfortable in the woods with her bow than in a ball gown, Merida would be perfectly content to ride her horse, Angus, around all day in the sunshine.

EYES AND BROW ARE
MORE ROUND

NO!   YES!

6

7

8

FOR MERIDA'S
HAIR, USE WILD,
SQUIGGLY LINES

Angus

Angus is Merida's trusty Clydesdale horse. Though he doesn't talk, he seems to understand Merida better than anyone else, and he plays with her and comforts her whenever she needs it.

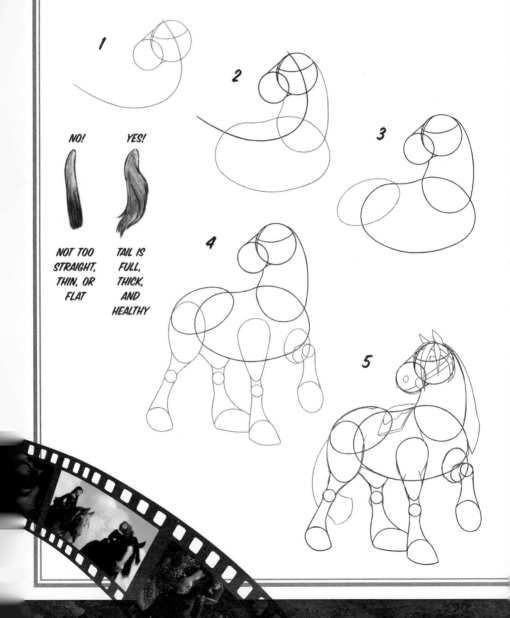

NO!

YES!

NOT TOO STRAIGHT, THIN, OR FLAT

TAIL IS FULL, THICK, AND HEALTHY

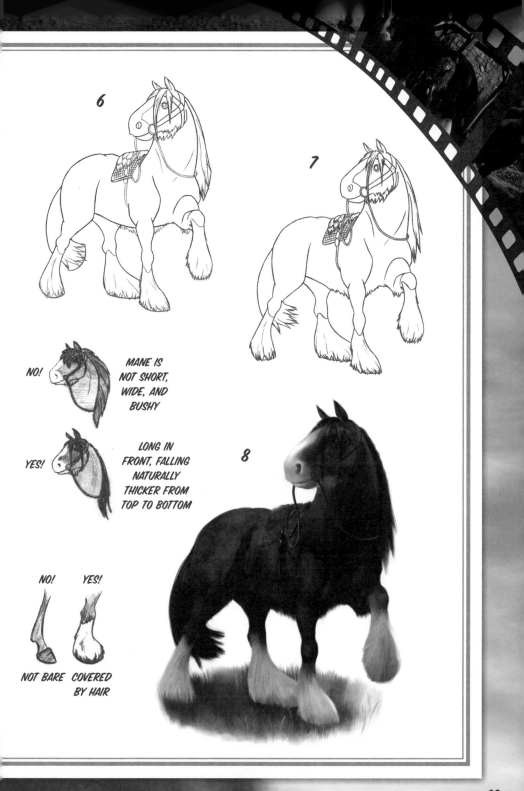

6

1

NO! MANE IS NOT SHORT, WIDE, AND BUSHY

YES! LONG IN FRONT, FALLING NATURALLY THICKER FROM TOP TO BOTTOM

8

NO! YES!

NOT BARE COVERED BY HAIR

Queen Elinor the Bear

Elinor is transformed into a bear when she eats a cake that the Witch gave to Merida. Merida and Elinor the Bear embark on a journey to find the Witch to change Elinor back, and in the process, mother and daughter grow closer than ever.

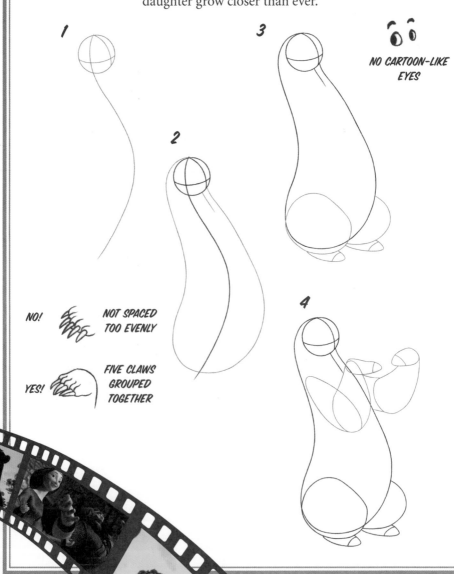

1

2

3

NO CARTOON-LIKE EYES

4

NO! NOT SPACED TOO EVENLY

YES! FIVE CLAWS GROUPED TOGETHER

5

6

7

8

King Fergus

An adventurer at heart, Fergus is always eager to teach his daughter, Merida, a thing or two on the bow and sword. Years ago, to save Elinor and Merida, Fergus fought the vicious bear Mor'du and lost his leg, but that hasn't dampened his jovial nature.

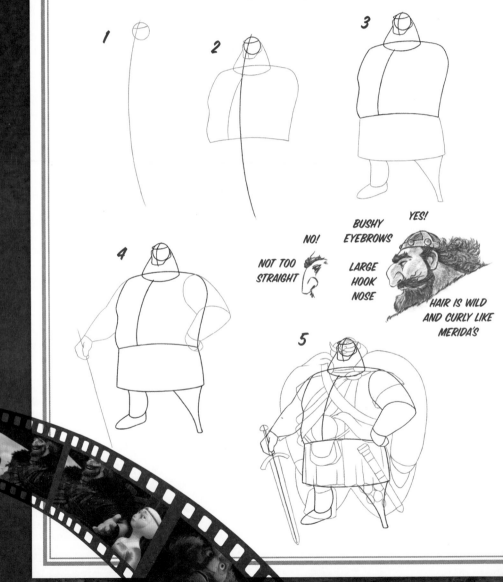

1

2

3

4

5

NO!

NOT TOO
STRAIGHT

BUSHY
EYEBROWS

YES!

LARGE
HOOK
NOSE

HAIR IS WILD
AND CURLY LIKE
MERIDA'S

6

7

NO!

YES!

NOT TOO
MANY STUDS

HELMET IS
SMALL

8

The Triplets

Harris, Hubert, and Hamish are Merida's identical-triplet brothers. Though they are troublemakers, they adore Merida and would do anything for her.

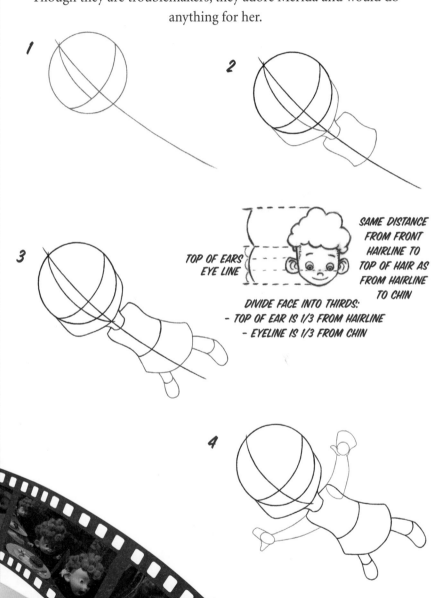

1

2

3

TOP OF EARS
EYE LINE

SAME DISTANCE
FROM FRONT
HAIRLINE TO
TOP OF HAIR AS
FROM HAIRLINE
TO CHIN

DIVIDE FACE INTO THIRDS:
- TOP OF EAR IS 1/3 FROM HAIRLINE
- EYELINE IS 1/3 FROM CHIN

4

5

6

7

A FEW
LOOSE HAIRS

CURLY HAIR
ON TOP, CUT
SHORT ON
THE SIDES

8

SKETCH HERE!

Woody

Woody is top toy in *Toy Story* and that's a tough spot to share, especially with a new toy named Buzz Lightyear, who thinks he's a real space ranger. But in *Toy Story 2*, Woody learns how to share the limelight with friends, both old and new. In *Toy Story 3*, Woody insists on making his way back to Andy, even though Andy has grown up.

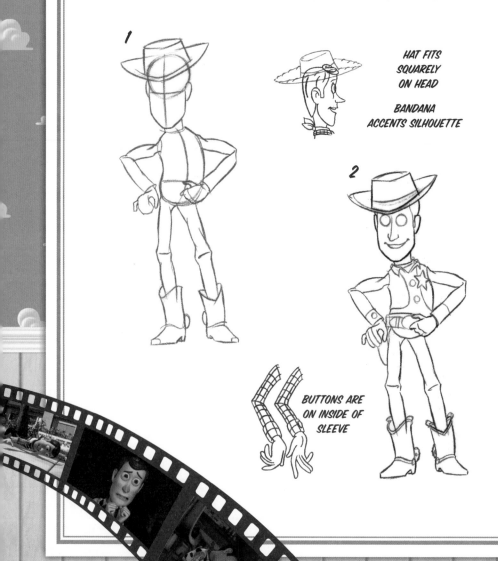

1

HAT FITS
SQUARELY
ON HEAD

BANDANA
ACCENTS SILHOUETTE

2

BUTTONS ARE
ON INSIDE OF
SLEEVE

3

WOODY IS ABOUT 4 HEADS TALL

BUCKLE HAS A STEER-HEAD DESIGN

SHERIFF BADGE IS A FIVE-POINT STAR

TOP VIEW OF WOODY'S HAT

THERE IS STITCHING AROUND THE EDGES

HAT BAND COMES UP 1/4 OF HAT HEIGHT

FOREARMS ARE LONGER THAN UPPER ARMS

CALVES ARE LONGER THAN THIGHS

EIGHT-POINTED SPURS

4

Buzz Lightyear

Buzz has stars in his eyes until Woody pulls him back down to Earth. For most of *Toy Story*, Buzz doesn't understand that he's a toy. But in *Toy Story 2*, he understands so well that he has to remind Woody. In *Toy Story 3*, Buzz is captured by a gang of hostile toys, who switch his setting to "demo." Woody and the others rescue him, but when they try to restore his setting, they accidentally switch his language button to Spanish!

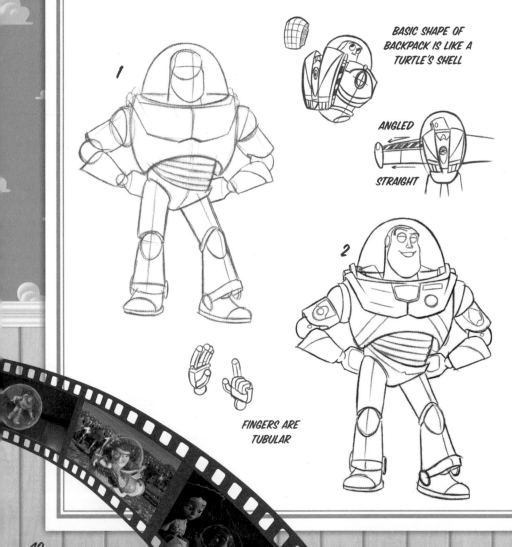

BASIC SHAPE OF BACKPACK IS LIKE A TURTLE'S SHELL

ANGLED

STRAIGHT

FINGERS ARE TUBULAR

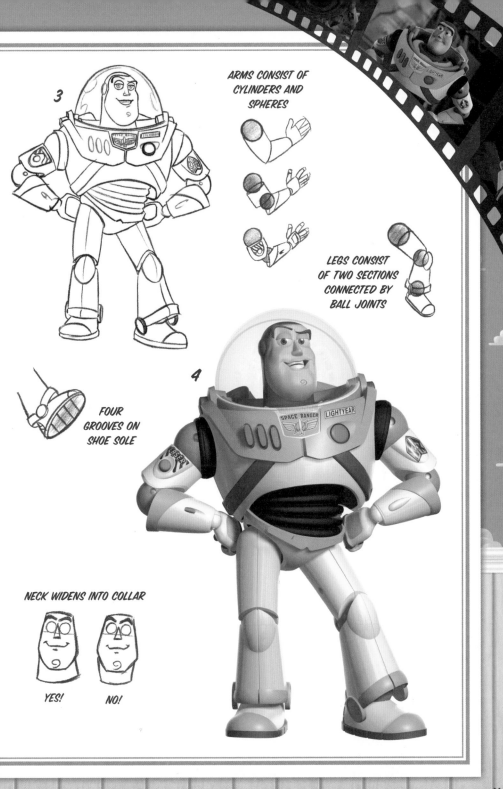

3

ARMS CONSIST OF CYLINDERS AND SPHERES

LEGS CONSIST OF TWO SECTIONS CONNECTED BY BALL JOINTS

4

FOUR GROOVES ON SHOE SOLE

SPACE RANGER LIGHTYEAR

NECK WIDENS INTO COLLAR

YES!   NO!

Bullseye

Bullseye, the sharpest horse in the West, is a trusty, energetic steed that loves Woody more than anything else in the world. This proud pony would do almost anything to keep his favorite sheriff out of harm's way.

1

YES! EYES SLANT APART SLIGHTLY

NO! NOT TOO MUCH

FOUR AND A HALF LOCKS GO DOWN LIKE A SAW BLADE

THREE LOCKS GO FORWARD

MOUTH IS LOW ON MUZZLE

HEAD IS CAPSULE-SHAPED

EARS ROLL LIKE FELT

2

3

BOTTOM
POINTS OF
TAIL LINE UP

TRY TO KEEP
A CLEAR LINE
OF ACTION

LEGS ARE LOOSE
AND FLOPPY

4

LEGS ARE TWO
STUFFED
SECTIONS,
ALMOST
SHAPED
LIKE PEANUTS

BOTTOM OF HOOF
IS SHAPED LIKE AN
UPSIDE-DOWN U

Rex

This toy dinosaur is one nervous Rex. When he's not worried about being replaced by a bigger dino toy, he's trying to avoid conflict in Andy's room. Rex's growl "almost" scares the other toys.

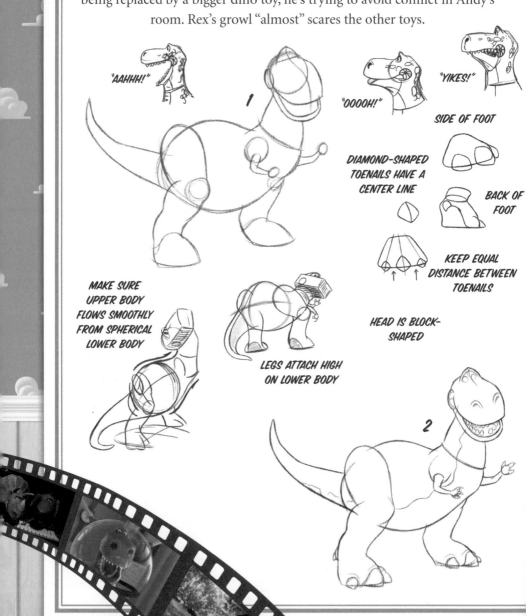

"AAHHH!"

1

"OOOOH!"

"YIKES!"

SIDE OF FOOT

DIAMOND-SHAPED TOENAILS HAVE A CENTER LINE

BACK OF FOOT

KEEP EQUAL DISTANCE BETWEEN TOENAILS

MAKE SURE UPPER BODY FLOWS SMOOTHLY FROM SPHERICAL LOWER BODY

LEGS ATTACH HIGH ON LOWER BODY

HEAD IS BLOCK-SHAPED

2

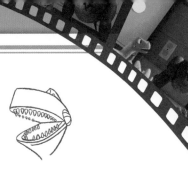

REX'S PUPILS ARE TINY.

BASIC EYE EXPRESSION

"HMMM."

"WHAT DID I STEP IN?"

"THE SKY IS FALLING!"

CONE-SHAPED TEETH

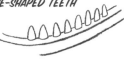

3

LEGS ARE THICK

4

ARMS ARE TINY WITH CLAWED FINGERS

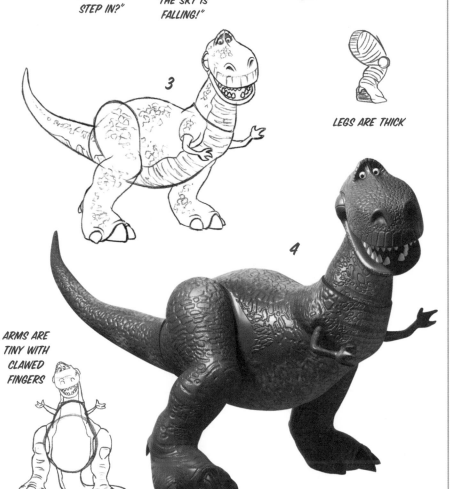

45

Mr. Potato Head

Mr. Potato Head can be cranky sometimes, but he's always there when Mrs. Potato Head needs another spud to lean on.

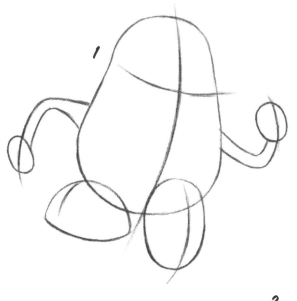

LARGE OVAL-SHAPED EYES

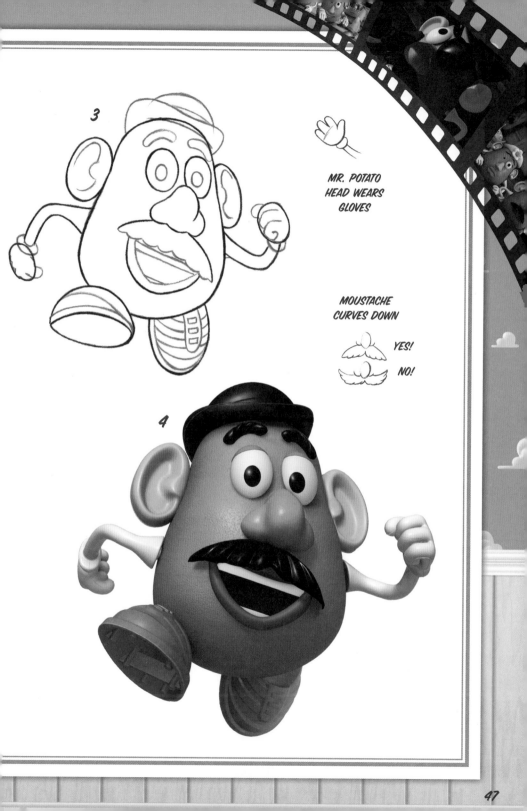

3

MR. POTATO
HEAD WEARS
GLOVES

MOUSTACHE
CURVES DOWN

YES!

NO!

4

Hamm

You can always count on Hamm to put in his two cents on any topic.
As Andy's piggy bank and Mr. Potato Head's buddy, Hamm says what
he thinks . . . especially when he thinks Woody's headed for trouble.

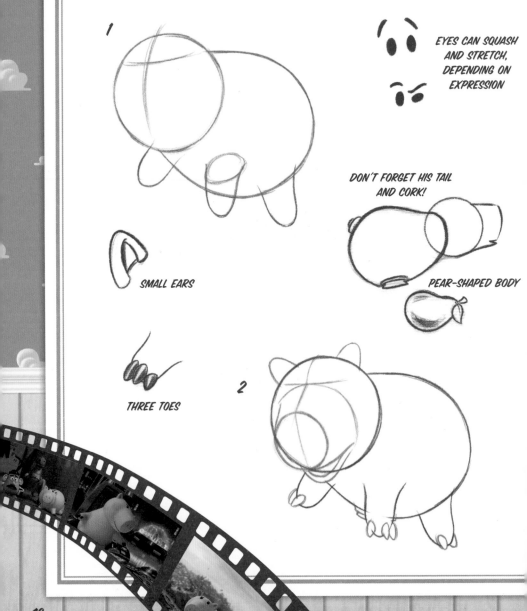

1

EYES CAN SQUASH
AND STRETCH,
DEPENDING ON
EXPRESSION

DON'T FORGET HIS TAIL
AND CORK!

SMALL EARS

PEAR-SHAPED BODY

THREE TOES

2

MOUTH IS A SMALL
SLIT ON BOTTOM
OF SNOUT

NOSE FITS ON
HEAD LIKE
A CUP ON A
SPHERE

3

HAMM'S COIN
SLOT

4

Jessie

Jessie knows what it means to be a toy. She once belonged to a little girl who loved her as much as Andy loves Woody. But that little girl gave Jessie away and in *Toy Story 2*, the brokenhearted cowgirl decides that being a collectible is better than being with a child who might outgrow you. Woody has to remind Jessie what being a toy is all about. In *Toy Story 3*, Jessie feels the same anxiety about being abandoned by her owner—but this time, it leads the whole gang to danger!

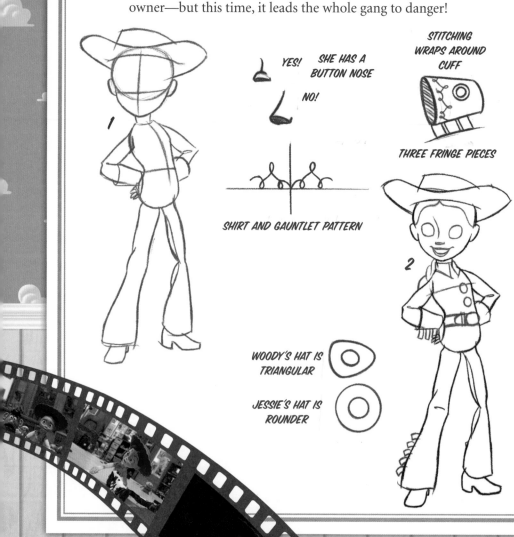

YES! SHE HAS A BUTTON NOSE

NO!

STITCHING WRAPS AROUND CUFF

THREE FRINGE PIECES

SHIRT AND GAUNTLET PATTERN

WOODY'S HAT IS TRIANGULAR

JESSIE'S HAT IS ROUNDER

3

4

HER HAT USUALLY
SITS ON THE BACK
OF HER HEAD

JESSIE'S BODY IS
FLEXIBLE LIKE A
RAG DOLL'S

The Prospector

The Prospector may seem like a nice grandfatherly type of fellow at first, but when his true feelings are revealed, it becomes clear that he's just plain selfish and mean. Having never belonged to a child, the Prospector simply doesn't know how to play—or be loved.

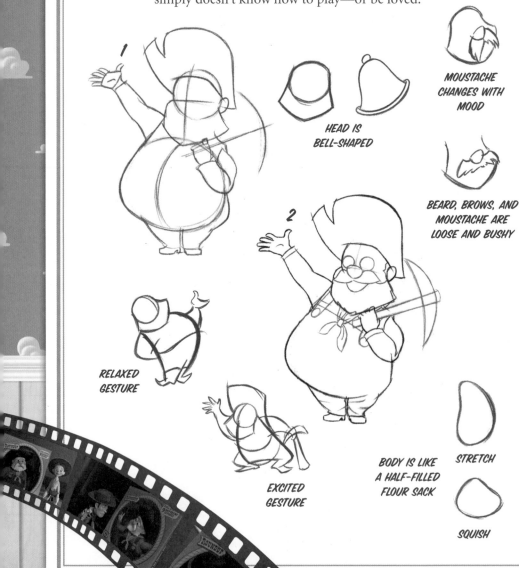

MOUSTACHE CHANGES WITH MOOD

HEAD IS BELL-SHAPED

BEARD, BROWS, AND MOUSTACHE ARE LOOSE AND BUSHY

RELAXED GESTURE

EXCITED GESTURE

BODY IS LIKE A HALF-FILLED FLOUR SACK

STRETCH

SQUISH

3

THE
PROSPECTOR
IS NEVER
WITHOUT HIS
PICKAXE

BOOT FLARES
AT TOP

BUTTON
DETAIL

HAT CURLS UP IN
FRONT AND BACK

POINTY
BEARD IN
SIDE VIEW

4

SMALL HANDS
WITH SLENDER
FINGERS

TIGHT-FITTING
SLEEVES

Slinky

"Slink" always has a spring in his step. He's a happy-go-lucky toy dog and one of Woody's strongest supporters. When Woody needs help, Slinky Dog goes the extra mile—or at least as far as he can stretch.

1

HE HAS ROUND EYES WITH THICK, HEAVY BROWS

HEAD IS A BALL

BACK LEGS HAVE BENDABLE KNEES

2

3

SLINKY IS A
PULL TOY, SO
HE HAS
A WHEEL ON
EACH FOOT

BODY IS TWO HALVES
OF A SPHERE ATTACHED
WITH A SPRING

EYE LIES
HALFWAY UP ON
HEAD CIRCLE

SPRING COMPRESSES
AND SHORTENS BODY

4

Aliens

It's a small world for the Alien toys at Pizza Planet. They live to see whom "the Claw" will pluck from their crane-game world. While trapped inside the crane game, the Aliens obey the Claw's calling, but once they leave, they happily switch their loyalty to others—like Mr. Potato Head, much to his chagrin.

3

4

Lotso

In *Toy Story 3*, Lots-o'-Huggin' Bear—a.k.a Lotso—seems like nothing more than the nicest teddy bear at Sunnyside Daycare. But Lotso's true colors are exposed when he traps Andy's toys in the Caterpillar Room with all of the rambunctious toddlers—and later when he leaves the toys to be incinerated at the garbage dump.

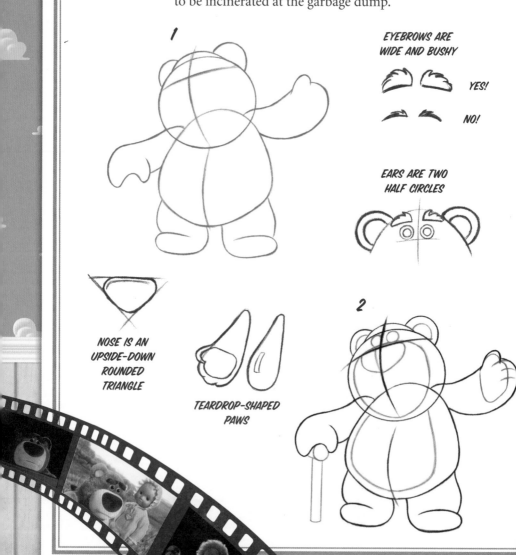

EYEBROWS ARE WIDE AND BUSHY

YES!

NO!

EARS ARE TWO HALF CIRCLES

NOSE IS AN UPSIDE-DOWN ROUNDED TRIANGLE

TEARDROP-SHAPED PAWS

1

2

3

EYES ARE
ROUND AND
SET CLOSE
TOGETHER

HIS CANE IS
A WOODEN
MALLET

4

SKETCH HERE!

Flik

Flik is a lovable worker ant whose inventions are often brilliant but disastrous. Clumsy and easily excited, Flik is known for his uncanny ability to make things go wrong. But his ideas are what ultimately save the ant colony from Hopper and his gang.

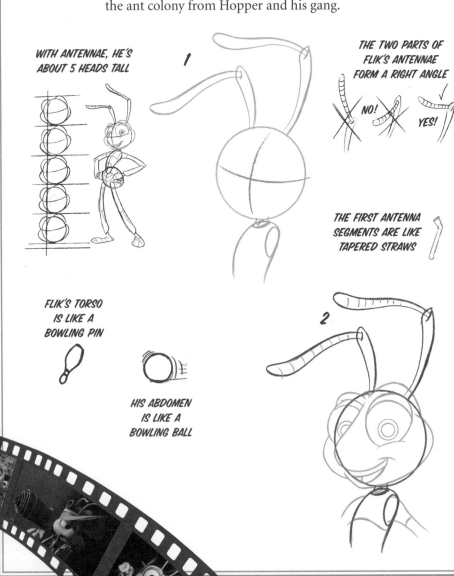

WITH ANTENNAE, HE'S
ABOUT 5 HEADS TALL

1

THE TWO PARTS OF
FLIK'S ANTENNAE
FORM A RIGHT ANGLE

NO!

YES!

THE FIRST ANTENNA
SEGMENTS ARE LIKE
TAPERED STRAWS

FLIK'S TORSO
IS LIKE A
BOWLING PIN

HIS ABDOMEN
IS LIKE A
BOWLING BALL

2

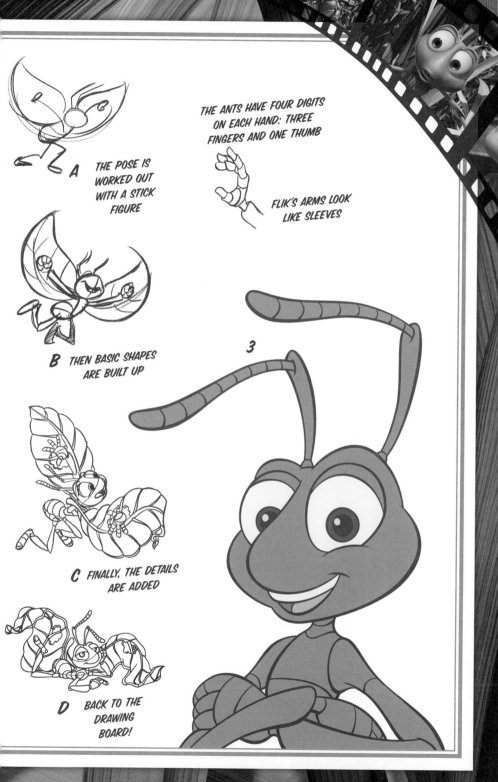

A THE POSE IS WORKED OUT WITH A STICK FIGURE

THE ANTS HAVE FOUR DIGITS ON EACH HAND: THREE FINGERS AND ONE THUMB

FLIK'S ARMS LOOK LIKE SLEEVES

B THEN BASIC SHAPES ARE BUILT UP

3

C FINALLY, THE DETAILS ARE ADDED

D BACK TO THE DRAWING BOARD!

Dot

Princess Dot is the adorable daughter of the Queen and little sister to Princess Atta. She is innocent and wide-eyed, but she is also spunky and tomboyish. Dot is the only one who believes in Flik during times of trouble.

THIS IS PRINCESS DOT'S BLUEBERRY UNIFORM. THE CAPE IS A LEAF.

DOT IS SHAPED A LOT LIKE YOU-KNOW-WHO

HER EYES SIT ON THE MIDLINE OF THE FACE

3

WITH ANTENNAE,
DOT IS JUST ABOUT
3½ HEADS TALL

EXPRESSIONS LIKE
THIS SHOW HER
PLUCKY ATTITUDE

WHEN POSING DOT,
THINK "FUN"

DOT HAS A ROUGHLY
ELLIPTICAL HEAD THAT
IS LARGE IN RELATION
TO HER BODY

BE CAREFUL WHEN DRAWING DOT'S
ANTENNAE. THEY POINT NEITHER AHEAD
NOR STRAIGHT TO THE SIDE

SKETCH HERE!

Sulley

"RRROAR!" Although Sulley scares kids for a living, he really has a heart of gold and is an all-around nice guy. Sulley's a gentle giant who would never hurt anyone—especially not a kid! When Sulley and Mike discover that scaring them might not be the best thing for kids, they decide to do something about it, which changes Monsters, Inc. forever.

1

OUTSIDE OF HORN HAS ANGLES; INSIDE IS CURVED

2

EYELID IS ROUNDED LIKE THIS · YES! · NO!

YES! EYEBROWS OVERLAP LIKE THIS . . .

. . . AND THIS

NO! NOT SEPARATED LIKE THIS

3

4

YES! BEND KNEES TO
SHOW WEIGHT

NO! DON'T MAKE
LEGS TOO STRAIGHT

DRAW BIG
HANDS WITH
POINTED
NAILS

5

YES!

NO!
DON'T ROUND
OUT TOES

Mike

As best friend and scare assistant to James P. Sullivan, Mike Wazowski is proud of his job, and he loves the perks that go along with it. Mike wouldn't change a thing about his life—except maybe to eliminate all the paperwork he has to do. A little green ball of energy, Mike is always ready with a joke and a smile, especially for his best girl, Celia.

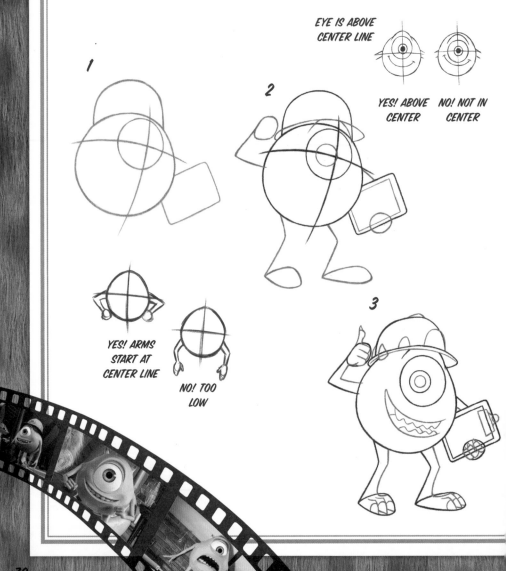

EYE IS ABOVE
CENTER LINE

YES! ABOVE   NO! NOT IN
CENTER   CENTER

1

2

YES! ARMS
START AT
CENTER LINE

NO! TOO
LOW

3

4

YES! LEGS ARE
BENT AND
SPACED APART

NO! NOT
STRAIGHT
AND CLOSE

YES! TEETH
ARE ROUNDED

NO! NOT
SHARP

5

Boo

Don't be scared—Boo is just the name that Sulley gave to the little girl who journeyed through her closet door into Monstropolis. Adorable and extremely curious, Boo isn't afraid of Mike and Sulley—but they're plenty afraid of her! Completely unaware that she might be in danger, Boo is in no rush to go back to the human world; she's having too much fun in Monstropolis!

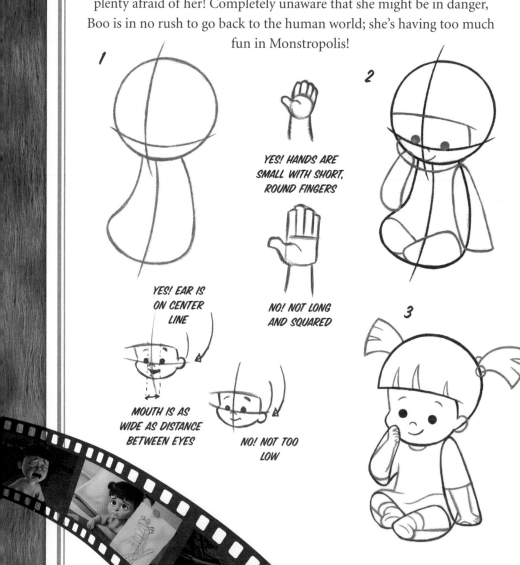

1

YES! HANDS ARE SMALL WITH SHORT, ROUND FINGERS

NO! NOT LONG AND SQUARED

2

YES! EAR IS ON CENTER LINE

MOUTH IS AS WIDE AS DISTANCE BETWEEN EYES

NO! NOT TOO LOW

3

4

YES! PIGTAILS
ARE ROUNDED

NO! NOT
STRAIGHT

5

YES!
BIG BREAKS
IN HAIR

NO!
NOT
LITTLE
TRIANGLES

SKETCH HERE!

Nemo

Here's Nemo—the adventurous little fish with the "lucky" fin who longs for excitement and friends to play with. Instead, he's saddled with an over-protective single dad who never lets the poor little guy out of his sight. When Nemo dares to show his friends he's not scared of the ocean (the way his dad is), he swims off alone, and he ends up getting a lot more excitement than he bargained for! But he also discovers just how brave and resourceful he can be.

1

2

FROM THE SIDE,
NEMO IS SHAPED
LIKE THIS

FROM FRONT,
BODY LOOKS
LIKE A
GUMDROP

3

YES! TOP
(DORSAL) FIN IS
TWO DIFFERENT
SHAPES, POINTING
AT DIFFERENT
ANGLES

NO! TOO
EVEN; TOO
UPRIGHT

4

YES! VARIED STRIPE SHAPES

NO! TOO SIMILAR AND TOO STRAIGHT

"LUCKY" FIN IS WEDGE-SHAPED WITH NOTCH CUT OUT

TOP FIN IS SAME HEIGHT AS ONE EYE

NEMO IS ABOUT 4 "EYES TALL," INCLUDING TOP FIN

YES! RAYS FOLLOW CURVE OF FIN

NO! TOO STRAIGHT AND EVEN

YES! BOTTOM FINS ARE SET APART FROM EACH OTHER

5

NO! FINS DON'T LOOK LIKE BOW TIE

Marlin

Marlin is Nemo's dad—the not-so-funny clownfish. After losing almost all of his family, Marlin has become overprotective of his only son. He fusses and frets a lot, but he really does mean well. It takes a little journey across the ocean to teach him the meaning of trust and letting go.

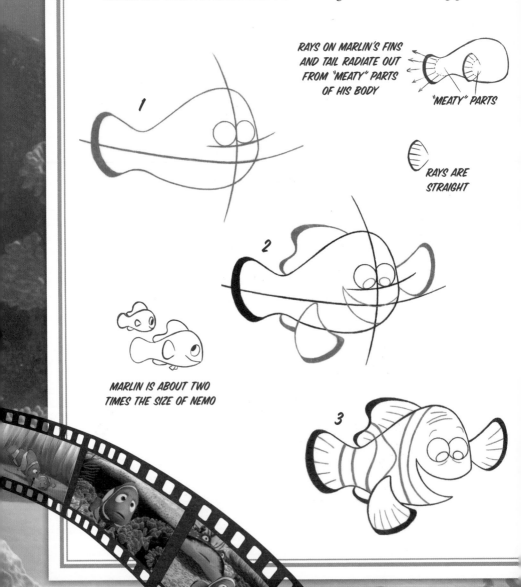

RAYS ON MARLIN'S FINS AND TAIL RADIATE OUT FROM "MEATY" PARTS OF HIS BODY

"MEATY" PARTS

RAYS ARE STRAIGHT

1

2

MARLIN IS ABOUT TWO TIMES THE SIZE OF NEMO

3

4

FACE IS KIND
OF FLAT

FIVE RAYS ON
SIDE (PECTORAL)
FINS AND TAIL

YES!
EYES ARE
CLOSE
TOGETHER

NO! EYES
ARE NOT
TOO FAR
APART

FROM THE SIDE, HE IS
SHAPED LIKE
A TURKEY
DRUMSTICK

5

BAGS UNDER
THE EYES
MAKE HIM
LOOK TIRED

Dory

Dory is one chatty, friendly, funny fish! She never gives up hope—when things get tough, she just keeps swimming. Always willing and helpful, Dory has everything going for her except for one small thing—her memory. She can't remember anything! But she risks her own life to help Marlin find Nemo.

1

2

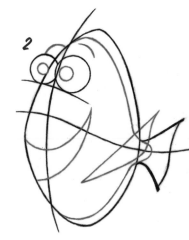

FROM THE FRONT, DORY'S STRIPE DEFINES WHERE HER "EYEBROWS" END

FRECKLES FOLLOW CURVED BRIDGE OF "NOSE"

YES! CURVED FRECKLE PATTERN

NO! FRECKLES AREN'T STRAIGHT

DORY IS JUST OVER FOUR TIMES THE SIZE OF NEMO

3

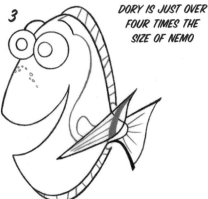

4

"EYEBROWS" FLOW
INTO CURVED
BODY PATTERN

YES! TAIL FIN IS
ONE S-SHAPED
CURVE

FIVE RAYS
ON TAIL

NO! TOO
MANY
RIPPLES

BIG EYES
NEAR TOP
OF THE
HEAD

EYES AND MOUTH
FORM UPSIDE-
DOWN TRIANGLE

SIDE (PECTORAL)
FINS START
NEAR THE BOTTOM
OF HER BODY AND
ANGLE UP

THIN BODY
FROM FRONT
VIEW

5

SIDE FINS
STRAIGHT ON
TOP . . .

THREE
RAYS

. . . CURVED
ON BOTTOM

FROM THE SIDE,
BODY IS SHAPED LIKE
A FOOTBALL

Gill

Gill is the leader of the Tank Gang—a group of fish trapped inside a tank in a dentist's office. He's charming, likable, tough, and determined to break his friends out of the tank. He takes Nemo under his "scarred" fin to teach him the ropes, and ultimately gives Nemo an important role in the great escape he's been planning for years.

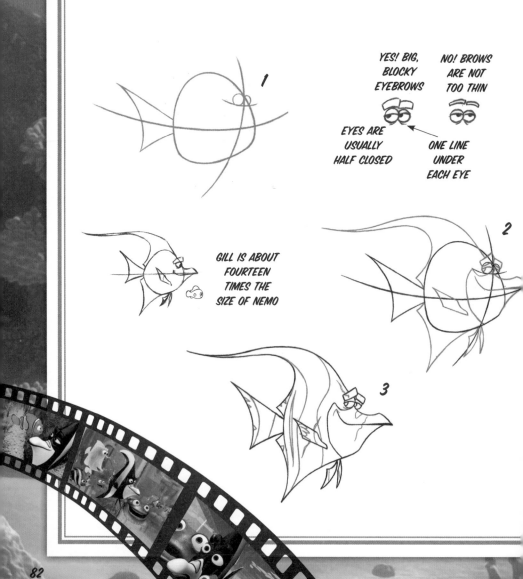

1

YES! BIG, BLOCKY EYEBROWS

NO! BROWS ARE NOT TOO THIN

EYES ARE USUALLY HALF CLOSED

ONE LINE UNDER EACH EYE

GILL IS ABOUT FOURTEEN TIMES THE SIZE OF NEMO

2

3

4

YES! TOP (DORSAL) FIN HAS AN ELEGANT CURVE

SCAR OVER EYEBROW

NO! TOO MANY CURVES

GILL HAS DEFINITE LIP

YES! SCAR ON FACE LOOKS LIKE THIS

NO! SCAR SHOULDN'T TOUCH EDGES

SCARRED FIN LOOKS TORN AND RAGGED

HAS SEVERAL SCARS

LEFT SIDE (PECTORAL) FIN HAS THIS SHAPE, WITH FIVE RAYS

5

TAIL FIN IS TRIANGULAR WITH THREE NOTCHES CUT OUT

Bubbles

Did you ever hear the saying, "life is just a bowl of bubbles?" Well for Bubbles, it is. This crazy fish is in love with bubbles. He faithfully waits for bubbles to burst from the tank's plastic treasure chest and then joyously scrambles to put them back in. He never tires of this game, and he keeps the other fish amused. For Bubbles, it's all about the bubbles.

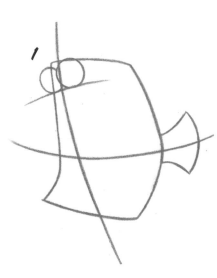

1

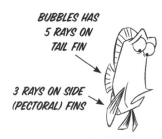

BUBBLES HAS 5 RAYS ON TAIL FIN

3 RAYS ON SIDE (PECTORAL) FINS

HAS EXAGGERATED EXPRESSIONS

BUBBLES IS ABOUT 2 TIMES AS WIDE AND 4 TIMES AS TALL AS NEMO

2

EYES SIT RIGHT AT TOP OF HEAD

EYEBROWS ARE EXPRESSIVE

4

3

YES! JUST SLIGHTLY ANGULAR TOP (DORSAL) FIN

NO! SHAPE TOO SMOOTH

5

EYELIDS ADD EXPRESSION TOO

SMILE PUSHES CHEEK UP TO OVERLAP EYE SLIGHTLY

SIDE FINS ARE LIKE ARMS—USED TO COLLECT BUBBLES

TOP LIP COMES TO POINT

YES! RAYS ON TOP FIN ARE IRREGULAR

NO! RAYS TOO EVENLY SPACED AND ALIGNED

85

Gurgle

Gurgle is a fussy little fish who refuses to touch anything around him. He's so afraid of germs that he is completely obsessed with them. He believes that if he steers clear of everything and everyone in the tank, his odds are better for a longer, happier life. How smart is that? Everybody knows that tank fish don't live forever, and Gurgle isn't taking any chances!

GURGLE'S BODY CURVES LIKE AN OBLONG WATER BALLOON

GURGLE IS ABOUT 2 TIMES THE SIZE OF NEMO

EYES SIT ON TOP
OF HEAD

IF FLAT, PATTERN
WOULD LOOK
LIKE THIS . . .

. . . BUT ON BODY,
PATTERN CURVES
AS IF WRAPPED
AROUND TUBE

YES! LIPS
ARE
ANGULAR

YES! ROUNDED
TAIL FIN

NO! TAIL FIN
TOO POINTED

NO! LIPS
TOO
ROUNDED

4

3

5

YES! PUPILS
ARE OVAL

NO! PUPILS
TOO ROUND

PUPILS GET
SMALLER
WHEN HE'S
SCARED

Peach

Meet Peach—the tank's star reporter. She spends day after day stuck up high on the glass wall of that tank. And what else is there to do but report back on everything she sees? Unfortunately life can be pretty boring in a dentist's office, except when the dentist is working on a patient. Peach has watched countless hours of dental procedures, so she is the tank's dental expert. She spends the rest of her days counting floor tiles and watching the plants die.

PEACH'S REFLECTION SHOWS ON GLASS AS SHE PULLS AWAY

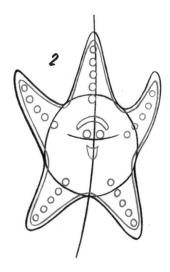

PEACH IS ABOUT 3 TIMES THE SIZE OF NEMO

YES! ANGLES AND POINTS ARE ROUNDED

NO! TOO SHARP

4

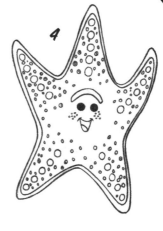

3

STAR POINTS WORK LIKE ARMS AND LEGS

EYES ARE SOLID BLACK CIRCLES

YES! SMALL SPOTS ARE VARIOUS SIZES AND IN UNEVEN PATTERN

5 MAIN CIRCLES FOR SUCTIONS ON EACH ARM (INSIDE)

NO! SPOTS TOO EVEN

5

EYEBROWS AND SHAPE OF EYES SHOW HER EXPRESSION

Jacques

Jacques is a true original. He is one shrimp who loves to clean. He would clean the tank from morning until night if he could—perhaps cleaning could help a fish relax a little. After all, everyone likes a nice clean reef! Jacques is like a good soldier: he's a born fighter, always doing battle with his greatest enemy—tank scum.

YES! EYES OVERLAP

NO! TOO FAR APART

1

JACQUES' FACIAL FEELERS RESEMBLE A MOUSTACHE

2

JACQUES IS JUST HALF THE SIZE OF NEMO

LEGS
SPIKY
AND
NOTCHED

"HANDS"
ARE LIKE
MITTS

4

3

 TAIL FIN HAS
1 LARGE SPOT

5

YES! THIN
DARK
STRIPES

 NO! DARK
STRIPES
TOO THICK

BODY ALWAYS
CURVES

SKETCH HERE!

Mr. Incredible

A man of super strength, Mr. Incredible was once the best-known, most popular Super alive! Then, through the Super Relocation Program, Mr. Incredible became "normal" Bob Parr, a claims adjuster at probably the worst insurance company ever. But Bob is not content with his ordinary life. He misses being a Super. Then one day, a mysterious summons calls the hero back to action.

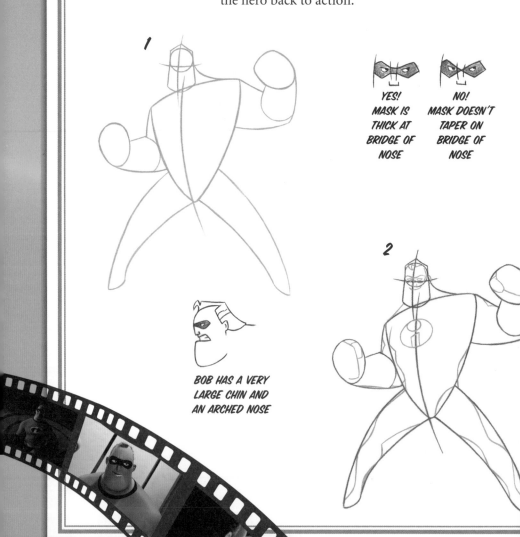

YES!
MASK IS
THICK AT
BRIDGE OF
NOSE

NO!
MASK DOESN'T
TAPER ON
BRIDGE OF
NOSE

BOB HAS A VERY
LARGE CHIN AND
AN ARCHED NOSE

1

2

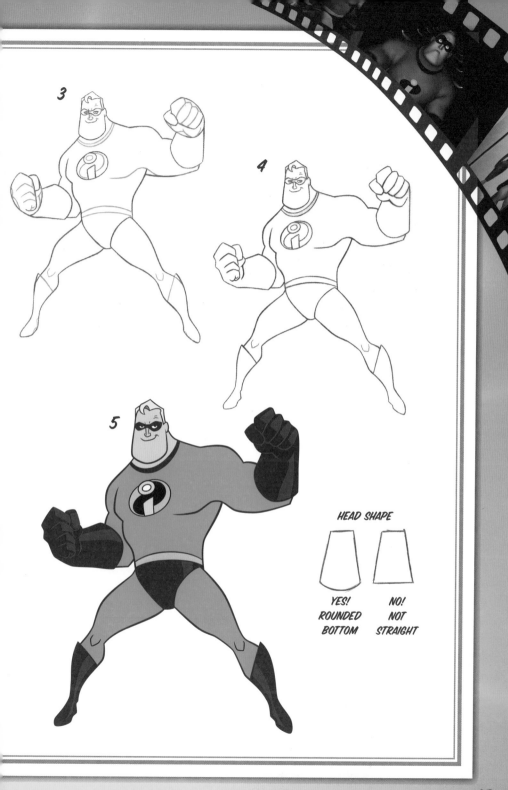

3

4

5

HEAD SHAPE

YES!
ROUNDED
BOTTOM

NO!
NOT
STRAIGHT

Elastigirl

No one is as flexible as Elastigirl, a Super with an incredible reach! She can stretch her arm and land a punch before the crooks know what hit them! But, as Helen Parr, Bob's wife and a mother of three, her Super powers are kept secret and largely unused—that is, until she finds out her Super spouse needs help! "Leave the saving of the world to the men? I don't think so!"

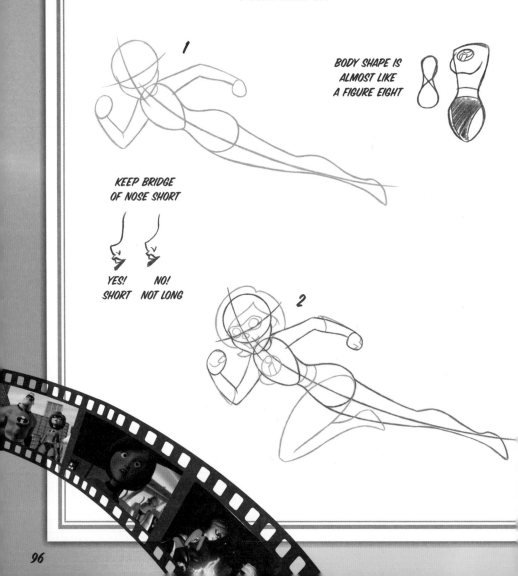

1

BODY SHAPE IS ALMOST LIKE A FIGURE EIGHT

KEEP BRIDGE OF NOSE SHORT

YES! SHORT   NO! NOT LONG

2

3

4

5

HELEN'S HAIR IS NOT
COMPLETELY ROUND—
THERE IS A SERIES OF
FLATTENED AREAS

FLAT FLAT FLAT FLAT

Frozone

Frozone was once known as the coolest Super on the planet. With the ability to create ice from the moisture in the air, he could build ice bridges, skate across them with special boots, and freeze criminals right in their tracks. Known as Lucius Best in his secret life, Frozone is also Mr. Incredible's best friend—and a reluctant partner in Bob's undercover heroics.

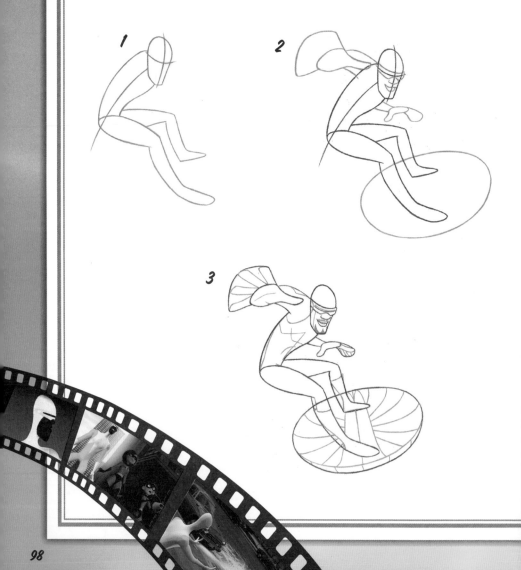

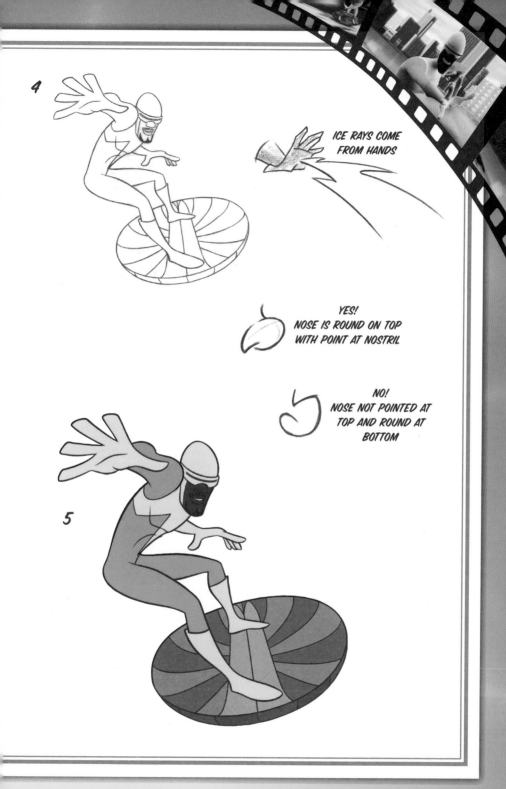

4

ICE RAYS COME
FROM HANDS

YES!
NOSE IS ROUND ON TOP
WITH POINT AT NOSTRIL

NO!
NOSE NOT POINTED AT
TOP AND ROUND AT
BOTTOM

5

SKETCH HERE!

Lightning McQueen

In *Cars*, Lightning McQueen is a hotshot rookie race car who cares only about two things: winning—and the fame and fortune that come with it. But all of that changes when he suddenly finds himself in the sleepy old town of Radiator Springs. In *Cars 2*, Lightning is a worldwide celebrity whose every dream has come true. Famous, successful, and surrounded by great friends, Lightning is ready to enjoy time in the slow lane—just as soon as he wins the World Grand Prix.

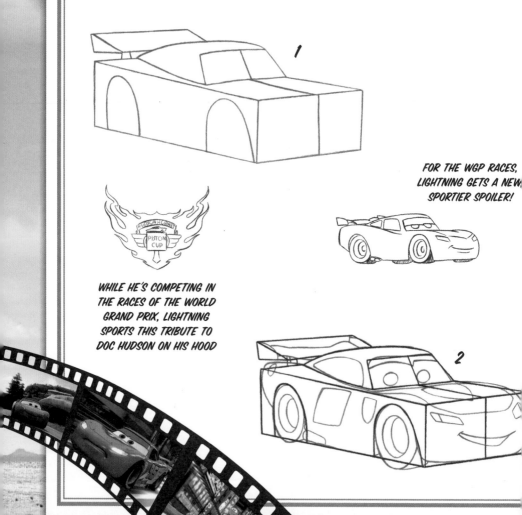

1

FOR THE WGP RACES, LIGHTNING GETS A NEW SPORTIER SPOILER!

WHILE HE'S COMPETING IN THE RACES OF THE WORLD GRAND PRIX, LIGHTNING SPORTS THIS TRIBUTE TO DOC HUDSON ON HIS HOOD

2

3

4

5

Mater

Mater is a friendly tow truck with a big heart, and he's always willing to lend a helping hook. He is the self-proclaimed world's best backward driver, who also gets a kick out of tractor tipping. In *Cars 2*, Mater gets caught up in a web of espionage when he accompanies Lightning to the World Grand Prix.

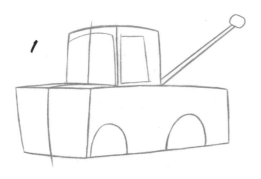

1

YES!   NO!

HIS MISSHAPEN BUCK-
TEETH AREN'T PERFECT
SQUARES—AND THERE'S A
GAP BETWEEN THEM

YES!
MIRRORS ARE
AT IRREGULAR
ANGLES

NO!
MIRRORS ARE
NOT PERFECTLY
ALIGNED

2

3

KEEP FACIAL EXPRESSIONS
OFF CENTER TO
EMPHASIZE MATER'S
GOOFINESS

YES! YES!

NO!
NOT
CENTERED

4

5

Sally

In *Cars*, Sally, a smart and beautiful sports car, is determined to restore Radiator Springs to the bustling town it was in its heyday. Originally an attorney from Los Angeles, she shows Lightning that sometimes it's good to live life in the slow lane. In *Cars 2*, Sally shows Lightning her support by showing up for the final leg of the World Grand Prix.

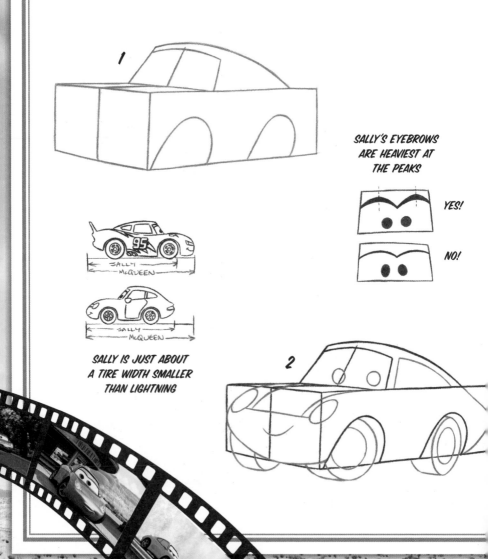

SALLY'S EYEBROWS ARE HEAVIEST AT THE PEAKS

YES!

NO!

SALLY
McQUEEN

SALLY
McQUEEN

SALLY IS JUST ABOUT A TIRE WIDTH SMALLER THAN LIGHTNING

3

4

YES!
SPOKES
HAVE A
CURVED
PATTERN

NO!
NOT
STRAIGHT

NO!
NOT
SHARP

5

Doc Hudson

Doc is a respected and admired town doctor, and he's the judge in Radiator Springs. But he has a mysterious past. Protective of the town, Doc cherishes the quiet and simple life. He wants nothing to do with the flashy race car Lightning McQueen.

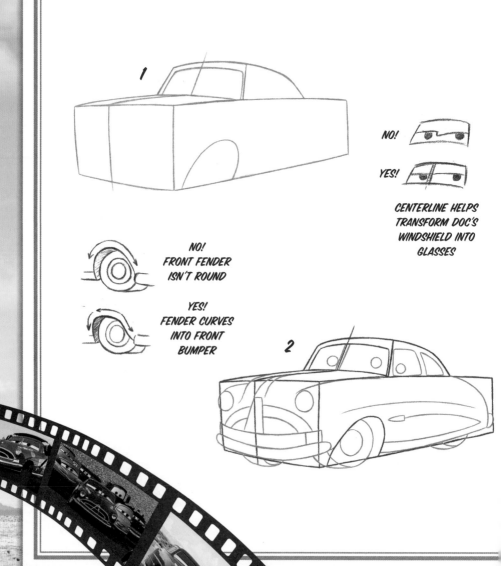

1

NO!

YES!

CENTERLINE HELPS
TRANSFORM DOC'S
WINDSHIELD INTO
GLASSES

NO!
FRONT FENDER
ISN'T ROUND

YES!
FENDER CURVES
INTO FRONT
BUMPER

2

3

4

DOC'S GRILLE IS LIKE A
RAINBOW BUILT OVER THE
CENTRAL LETTER A

5

Finn McMissile

British agent Finn McMissile is sleek, charming, intelligent, and loaded with cool gadgets! Finn knows there's a conspiracy afoot at the World Grand Prix. With the help of fellow British agent Holley Shiftwell—and Mater—he and his colleagues are destined to uncover the plot.

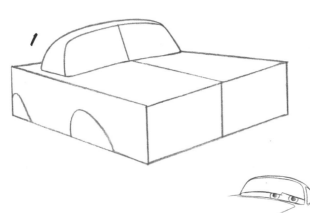

HE HAS LARGE TOP TEETH, WHICH SHOULD BE THE PREDOMINANT FEATURE IN HIS MOUTH

WHEN HIS PUPILS ARE SLIGHTLY COVERED BY HIS EYELIDS, IT CONVEYS HOW COOL HE LOOKS

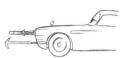

FINN HAS A BUILT-IN MISSILE LAUNCHER AND CAN FIRE GRAPPLING HOOKS

3

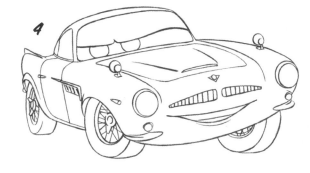

4

FINN CAN
TRANSFORM INTO
A HYDROPLANE

5

Francesco Bernoulli

International racing champ Francesco Bernoulli loves a good, clean race—almost as much as he adores himself. Francesco challenges Lightning McQueen to participate in the World Grand Prix. He even wins the first leg! Arrivederci!

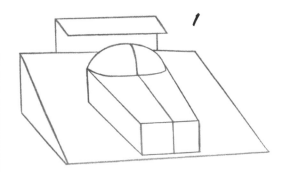

1

FRANCESCO'S "HEAD" WORKS LIKE A HELMET SITTING DOWN INTO THE BODY WITH THE AIR INTAKE ABOVE

YES!

NO!

BECAUSE HIS MOUTH IS SO FAR AWAY FROM HIS EYES, HIS EXPRESSIONS WILL READ MORE EASILY WHEN HE'S TURNED MORE TOWARD US RATHER THAN TO THE SIDE

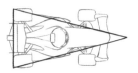

HIS BASIC BODY SHAPE IS A WEDGE THAT SLICES THROUGH THE AIR FOR MAXIMUM SPEED!

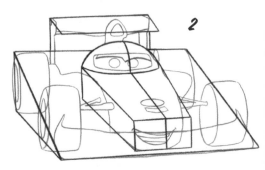

2

3

4

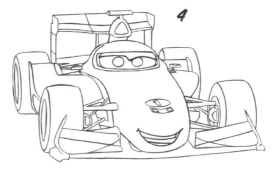

FRANCESCO SITS LOWER TO THE
GROUND THAN LIGHTNING

5

Professor Z

The savvy mad scientist Professor Z has mastered the art of sophisticated weapons design and has created an elaborate device disguised as a camera that can harm cars without leaving a trace of evidence. His goal—to sabotage the World Grand Prix racers.

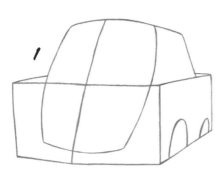

1

PROFESSOR Z IS REALLY SMALL

PROFESSOR Z LOOKS THE SAME COMING OR GOING!

HIS BROKEN ROOF RACK GIVES THE APPEARANCE OF A HAIR COMB-OVER

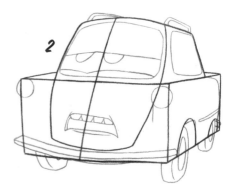

2

3

4

5

BE CAREFUL WHEN
POSING PROFESSOR Z
THAT HIS BODY
ANGLE DOESN'T
CAUSE HIS EYE TO
BE CUT ACROSS BY
HIS MONOCLE

YES!

NO!

Remy

Remy is a little rat with big dreams. Born with a highly developed sense of smell, he can't stand eating garbage like the other rats, and he longs to become a gourmet chef. When Remy accidentally lands in the late, great Chef Auguste Gusteau's famous restaurant, Remy's dream just might come true . . . if he can remain hidden.

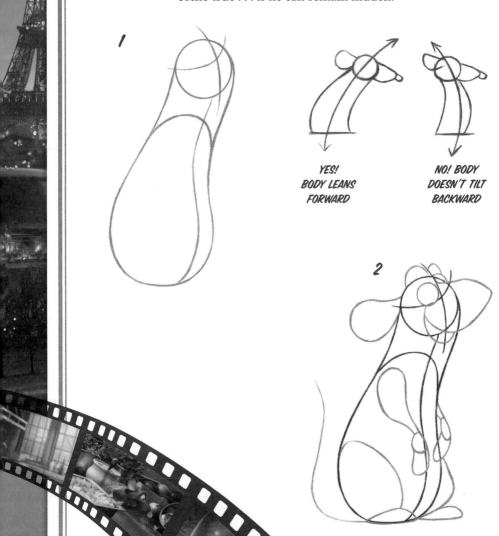

1

YES!
BODY LEANS
FORWARD

NO! BODY
DOESN'T TILT
BACKWARD

2

ARM HAIR IS RAGGED AND LOOSE

3

4

5

YES!
LEGS MERGE
WITH BODY
FOR A
RELAXED LOOK

NO!
LEGS ARE NOT
SEPARATE
SHAPES

Linguini

Linguini begins work at Gusteau's restaurant as a garbage boy, but an unexpected meeting with Remy gives him the chance to become a chef. Clumsy and timid, Linguini is an unlikely cook—especially because he knows nothing about cooking! Could his strange partnership with Remy actually succeed? *Mais oui!*

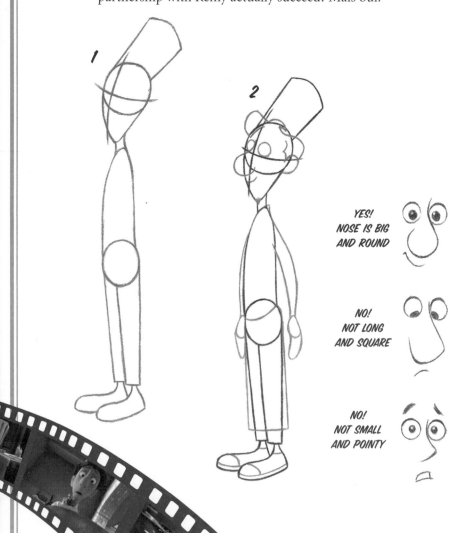

1

2

YES!
NOSE IS BIG
AND ROUND

NO!
NOT LONG
AND SQUARE

NO!
NOT SMALL
AND POINTY

3

4

5

YES!
LINGUINI HAS
FOUR FINGERS
AND A THUMB

SKETCH HERE!

WALL·E

WALL·E is a Waste Allocation Load Lifter—Earth class.
Although considered a bit ancient for the twenty-ninth century,
WALL·E is programmed with a strong directive: to collect and compact
trash to clean up the overly polluted Earth. His boxy middle contains
his compacting unit; his mechanical arms were designed to gather trash;
and his triangular-shaped treads cover the wheels that help him
maneuver over the rugged, trash-covered terrain.

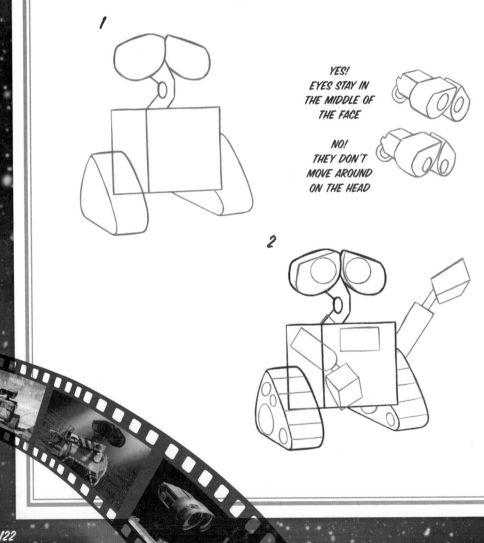

**YES!
EYES STAY IN
THE MIDDLE OF
THE FACE**

**NO!
THEY DON'T
MOVE AROUND
ON THE HEAD**

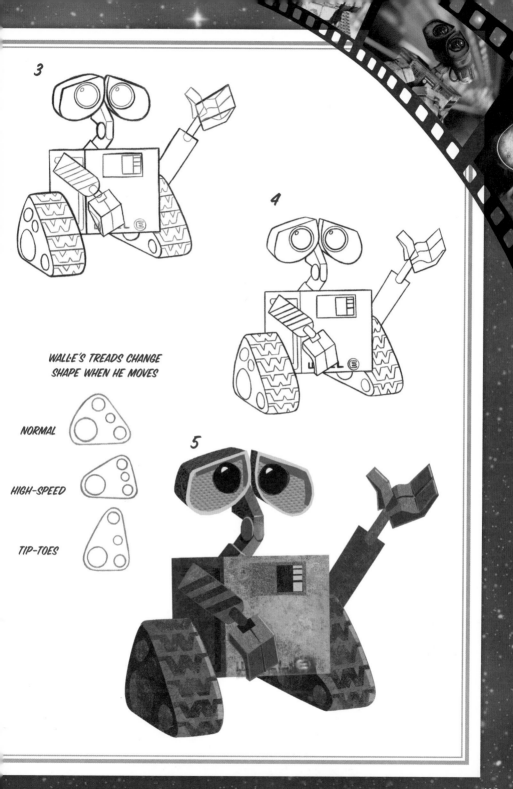

3

4

WALL·E'S TREADS CHANGE SHAPE WHEN HE MOVES

NORMAL

HIGH-SPEED

TIP-TOES

5

EVE

EVE is a probe-bot—an Extraterrestrial Vegetation Evaluator.
She was programmed with the directive to find vegetation on Earth.
If she finds a single plant on Earth, humans can return from
their space travels and live on Earth again.

FACIAL EXPRESSIONS

1

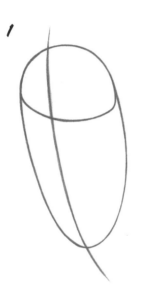

 NEUTRAL

 SKEPTICAL

 WORRIED OR SAD

 LAUGHING

2

CHEST
COMPARTMENT
CAN OPEN

3

4

5

EVE CAN DEFEND
HERSELF ON A
MOMENT'S NOTICE

EVE CAN GROW
FINGERS WHEN
NECESSARY

SKETCH HERE!

Credits